Fiction Teacher's Book 6
Wendy Body

Series Editor: Wendy Body

Pearson Education Limited
Edinburgh Gate
Harlow
Essex
CM20 2JE
England and Associated Companies throughout the World

ISBN 0582 48846 X
First published 2001
Second impression 2002

Printed in Great Britain by Scotprint, Haddington
Designed by AMR, Bramley, Hants

The Publisher's policy is to use paper manufactured from sustainable forests.

Edinburgh Gate
Harlow, Essex

If you wish to enlarge any of the Shared Writing Examples for use in your teaching, you may do so.

Contents

Year 6 Fiction Summary Chart

Unit in Resource Book	Text level objective	Sentence level objective links	Unit of work
Term 1 Unit 1 *Chimney-sweep!*	**T6**: to manipulate narrative perspective by writing in the voice and style of a text	**S5**: to form complex sentences through e.g. using different connecting devices	Rewrite from another character's view
Term 1 Unit 2 *Chimney-sweep!*	**T6**: to manipulate narrative perspective by producing a modern retelling	**S6**: to secure knowledge and understanding of more sophisticated punctuation marks	Write a modern retelling
Term 1 Unit 3 *Chimney-sweep!*	**T9**: to prepare a short section of story as a script, e.g. using stage directions, location/ setting		Write as a playscript
Term 1 Unit 4 Planning a story	**T7**: to plan quicly and effectively the plot, characters and structure of their own narrative writing	**S2**: ... to transform a sentence from active to passive and vice versa	Plan a story
Term 1 Unit 5 Planning a story	**T6**: to manipulate narrative perspective by writing a story with two different narrators		Write the story with two narrators
Term 1 Unit 6 *Oberon's Magic*	**T8**: to summarise a passage, chapter or text in a specified number of words	**S5**: to form complex sentences, e.g. through using different connecting devices ... exploring how meaning is affected by the sequence and structure of clauses	Write a summary
Term 1 Unit 7 *Death of a Snowman*	**T10**: to write own poem experimenting with active verbs and personification; produce revised poems for reading aloud individually	**S2**: to revise earlier work on verbs and to understand the terms *active* and *passive*	Using personification
Term 2 Unit 8 *Bones!*	**T10**: to use different genres as models to write, e.g. short extracts, sequels ... using appropriate conventions, language	**S1**: to identify examples of active and passive verbs in texts	Write the next episode
Term 2 Unit 9 Writing a Flashback Story	**T11**: to write own story using, e.g. flashbacks or a story within a story to convey the passing of time		Write a story using flashbacks

Term 2 Unit 10 Revising Your Writing	**T12**: to study in depth one genre and produce an extended piece of similar writing ... to revise, re-draft	**S3**: to revise work on complex sentences ... constructing complex sentences; appropriate use of punctuation	Revise own writing
Term 2 Unit 11 *Captain Hook's Plan*	**T13**: parody a literary text, describing stock characters and plot structure, language etc.	**S3**: to revise work on complex sentences ... constructing complex sentences; appropriate use of punctuation	Write a parody
Term 2 Unit 12 *Ute Prayer*	**T14**: to write commentaries or summaries crediting views expressed by using expressions such as 'The writer says that ...		Write a commentary
Term 3 Unit 13 *Meeting*	**T7**: to annotate passages in detail in response to specific questions		Annotate text
Term 3 Unit 14 *Meeting*	**T8**: to use a reading journal effectively to raise and refine personal responses to a text and prepare for discussion		Write an entry in a reading journal
Term 3 Unit 15 *Meeting*	**T12**: to compare texts in writing, drawing out their different styles and preoccupations; their strengths and weaknesses ...	**S1**: to revise the language conventions and grammatical features of the different types of text such as narrative ...	Compare texts in writing
Term 3 Unit 16 *River Cinquains*	**T13**: to write a sequence of poems linked by theme or form		Write a sequence of poems
Term 3 Unit 17 *Reunion*	**T9**: to write summaries of books or parts of books ...		Write a summary
Term 3 Unit 18 *Reunion*	**T11**: to write a brief helpful review tailored for real audiences	**S1**: to revise the language conventions and grammatical features of the different types of text	Write a brief review
Term 3 Unit 19 *Reunion*	**T10**: to write a brief synopsis of a text, e.g. for back cover blurb	**S4**: to secure control of complex sentences ...	Write a back cover blurb
Term 3 Unit 20 *Strange Meeting*	**T14**: to write an extended story, worked on over time		Write a plan for an extended story

Introduction

What Is *Pelican Shared Writing*?

Pelican Shared Writing is an easy-to-use resource for teaching shared writing. It comprises ten packs: one Fiction and one Non-Fiction pack for each year group for Years 2, 3, 4, 5 and 6. Each pack contains:
- one *Writing Resource Book*
- one *Teacher's Book* with copymasters
- a large sheet of acetate and a Pelican page clip

Each *Writing Resource Book* offers 20 units of work which cover all the NLS writing composition objectives for the year group. Each writing composition objective forms one unit of work. Links are also made to appropriate sentence level objectives.

Although *Pelican Shared Writing* stands alone, it has links to *Pelican Guided Reading and Writing* in terms of objectives and tasks and there are content links to *Pelican Big Books*.

The *Writing Resource Books*
- Each 48-page big book is split into three parts – one for each term's teaching objectives.
- Shared writing is rooted in shared reading, and so the *Writing Resource Books* contain the texts which not only provide the starting point for writing, but also act as models of the genre to be studied. Story plans and writing frames are sometimes included as well.
- Quotes about the writing process from professional children's writers feature on the inside back cover of some of the *Fiction Writing Resource Books* to initiate discussions on writing.
- Each book comes with a large sheet of acetate and a Pelican page clip for text marking and writing.

The *Teacher's Books*
The *Teacher's Book* in each pack contains:
- teaching pages for each unit of work with detailed, step-by-step advice on what to do for each shared writing session. There are also examples of completed activities which teachers can use to guide the class in composing a text. Units will usually take more than one shared writing session to complete.
- a small number of copymasters e.g. writing frames, character planners. These are for general use and can also be applied to other texts and writing activities
- copymaster versions of all the *Writing Resource Book* texts. These can be used to make overhead transparencies and in instances where it is helpful for children to have their own copy of a text e.g. for annotation.

The *Non-Fiction Writing Books* have a summary of links to other areas of the curriculum on the last page.

Teaching Shared Writing

Pelican Shared Writing complements the National Literacy Strategy's *Grammar for Writing* guidance. *Pelican Shared Writing* concentrates on delivering the text level writing composition objectives whereas *Grammar for Writing* concentrates on sentence level objectives. *Pelican Shared Writing* adopts a similar approach to shared writing which may be summarised as follows:

Key features of shared writing
- Make explicit how purpose and audience determine form and style.
- Link the writing to specific objectives.
- Rehearse sentences orally before writing.
- Discuss and explain alternatives and choices.
- Keep re-reading to maintain flow, meaning and consistency.
- Involve children in the revision and editing.

Shared Writing Techniques:

Teacher demonstration

The teacher composes and writes, modelling for children how to compose a particular text type or tackle a writing activity. He/she thinks aloud; rehearses choices before writing; explains choices and makes changes. The children do not contribute to the composition but they are invited to offer opinions on, for example, the choice of words or sentence construction. Demonstration time will vary according to the text and children's competence, but avoid spending too long – children need to try things for themselves.

Teacher scribing

The teacher acts as scribe and builds on the initial demonstration by getting the children to make contributions to the composition or task. The teacher guides, focuses, explains and challenges the contributions e.g. *Why did you choose that word? That's a really good sentence construction because …* While children could make their contributions orally by putting up their hands, it is preferable for them to use whiteboards (in pairs or individually) which ensures participation by all children. It is also advisable to take "time out" i.e. get children to turn to each other in pairs and discuss possibilities for 30 seconds or so.

Supported composition

Supported composition is preparation for independent writing. Children compose a limited amount of text using whiteboards or notebooks – in pairs or individually. Their alternatives are reviewed and discussed and choices and changes made. Some differentiation can be achieved by seating children in their ability groups and asking one group to compose one sentence orally, another to write one or two sentences and a third to write several sentences. Supported composition will enable you to identify those children who will need to repeat or continue the task in guided writing i.e. those who need greater support.

Shared writing is the most powerful means of improving and developing children's writing skills. But they will not develop into proficient writers unless, firstly, they are given sufficient TIME to practise the skills and craft of writing for themselves, and secondly, they receive the FEEDBACK which will help them evaluate what they have done and learn from it.

Teaching a *Pelican Shared Writing* unit of work

Support for each step will be found on the teaching pages

Discussing the Text for each unit

- Introduce the task and the objective
- Read the text in the Resource Book with the class and discuss the content
- Draw out features of the genre

Shared Writing

- Demonstrate or model the particular features of the writing
- Scribe and guide the pupils' contributions
- Continue with supported composition by children working in pairs
- Check the children's learning

Independent Writing

- Children complete the writing task.
- They consolidate their learning by carrying out another similar task.

Checking the Objective

- Determine children's understanding of the objective and how far they can apply their knowledge by evaluating their writing.

Revisiting the Objective

- If needs be, repeat the whole process using the suggested activity.

Note: A *Pelican Shared Writing* CD-ROM is available for use alongside each year's work. For further details, please see the section on ICT overleaf.

ICT and *Pelican Shared Writing*

ICT may be used by all pupils to support writing skills. The word processor or desktop publishing package can enable the child to focus on the development of ideas and the manipulation of the written word without the physical constraints imposed by the handwriting process. The ease of editing, the spell-checking facilities and the ability to move text around the page make ICT support programs valuable tools to include within the writing repertoire. Writing tasks offer the ideal opportunity to integrate and apply those ICT skills being developed in the ICT curriculum.

Almost any writing task may be approached using ICT as an optional writing tool. These writing tasks will offer strong links with the ICT curriculum, which aims for pupils to:

- 'develop their ability to apply their IT capability ICT to support their use of language and communication'
- 'pass on ideas by communicating, presenting and exchanging information'
- 'develop language skills eg in systematic writing and in presenting their own ideas'
- 'be creative and persistent'
- 'explore their attitudes towards ITC, its value for themselves ... and their awareness of its advantages and limitations'

(QCA Scheme of Work for ICT, Aims and Purposes)

The 'Communicating' strand for ICT is inextricably linked with developing literacy. Computer access is a great resource for independent, group and class work, and is too valuable a tool to remain unused during the development of literacy skills. It is a great motivator and encourages collaborative work that can become more focused as children's attention is extended.

Within the suggested Year 6 Non Fiction *Pelican Shared Writing* activities, there are some clear links with Unit 4A 'Writing for Different Audiences', from the QCA Scheme of Work for ICT. This unit focuses on text manipulation skills. The writing activities offer ideal opportunities for the application of these ICT sckills. If a multimedia authoring package is used, then the link to Unit 6A 'Multimedia Presentations' is made.

Links to the most relevant objectives from the National Curriculum Programme of Study for ICT are listed in the table opposite.

The differentiated writing frames for Year 6 (Fiction and Non-Fiction) are available on the CD-ROM entitled *Pelican Shared Writing Year 6* (ISBN 0582 50955 6), which can be easily installed on any machine supporting Microsoft Word. Here they may be adapted, should you so wish, to suit your particular needs. The CD-ROM also provides cross-referencing charts for both Writing and ICT targets, including the ICT Programme of Study references and links to the QCA Scheme of Work for ICT – collated and readily available for inclusion in planning records.

Year 6 Fiction
Relevant objectives from the ICT Programme of Study

Pupils should be taught:

1a
to talk about what information they need and how they can find and use it (*for example, searching the internet or a CD-ROM, using printed material, asking people*)

2a
how to develop and refine ideas by bringing together, organising and reorganising text, tables, images and sound as appropriate (*for example, desktop publishing, multimedia presentations*)

3a
how to share and exchange information in a variety of forms, including e-mail (*for example, displays, posters, animations, musical compositions*)

3b
to be sensitive to the needs of the audience and think carefully about the content and quality when communicating information (*for example, work for presentation to other pupils, writing for parents, publishing on the internet*).

4a
to review what they and others have done to help them develop their ideas

4b
describe and talk about the effectiveness of their work with ICT, comparing it with other methods and considering the effect it has on others (*for example, the impact made by a desktop-published newsletter or poster*)

National Curriculum for England, ICT Programmes of Study

Rewrite from another character's view

Writing objective

T6: To manipulate narrative perspective by writing in the voice and style of a text.

Links to sentence/word level work

S5: To form complex sentences through e.g. using different connecting devices.

Text Copymasters: C4–7

Discussing the Text

- Tell the children that the text 'Chimney-sweep' is taken from 'The Water Babies', written by Charles Kingsley in Victorian times.
- Read the extract to the children. *What is the setting?* (a school) *What can we tell about the character and behaviour of the dame* (teacher)?
- Discuss the language the author used, i.e. (1) Grammar differences, e.g. 'And how got ye up there?', 'Where didst come from?' (2) Vocabulary differences, e.g. Use of 'Thee' and 'Thou', 'ye'; 'clemmed', 'I'll warrant' (3) The use of dialect when the dame speaks, e.g. 'beck', 'bairn'.
- Points of style to discuss:
  – the use of dialect in speech
  – mainly short sentences and phrases in the dialogue
  – connectives – mainly 'and' to join clauses, also 'And' at the beginning of sentences. *Why do you think the author uses 'and' so much?* (Kingsley was writing for young children. It indicates his opinion on how to write for children.)

Shared Writing

For this session, keep the text on display, for reference.

Teacher demonstration

- Tell the children that you are going to write in the style of 'The Water Babies' by rewriting Tom's appearance at the school from the point of view of one of the children. Together decide which it will be. (The example provided is from a boy's point of view.) *What would the boys (or girls) have thought and felt, seeing Tom at the door?*
- *The opening sentence will set the scene and be in the first person.* Write the first sentence (see Shared Writing Example Paragraph 1).
- *Now I am going to describe Tom from the boy's point of view.* Write the second sentence, commenting on your choice of language as you write, e.g. *What language would he have used? Scruffy? Ragged? Ragamuffin? Urchin?*
- As you write the third sentence about the boys' and girls' reactions (see Example), comment on appropriate adjectives for the time and how you might drop in a clause to explain the girls' or boys' behaviour, e.g. 'being timid creatures'. Talk through the punctuation you use to connect the clauses.

Teacher scribing

- Tell the children that together you are going to compose the next paragraph about the first conversation between Tom and the dame. *We need to write about the teacher next. What shall we call her?* Agree a name and suitable form of address, e.g. Mistress Braithwaite.

- *What was the dame's first reaction to Tom?* (page 2) *How would one of the boys write about it? Will we use direct or reported speech?* Write the paragraph, taking suggestions from the class and adjusting the language to fit the style and voice of the text. (See Shared Writing Example Paragraph 2, below.)

Shared Writing Example

Paragraph 1

We were sitting in our places on the bench and working hard at our times tables when, all of a sudden, Benjamin Tompkins laughed. I looked up to see a ragged, black-faced urchin in the doorway. It was such an odd sight that all we boys joined in the laughter but some of the girls, being timid creatures, started to cry.

Paragraph 2

And Mistress Braithwaite, seeing the intruder to be a chimney-sweep, was angry and told him to be off. She is most strict with us and we dare not disobey her but, to my astonishment, this ragamuffin answered her back and begged her for a drink of water. She told him to go down to the beck, but he slumped down on the door-step, motionless.

Supported composition
- Re-read the next part of the story. *How did the dame's attitude to Tom change? What did she do?* Ask the children to write two or three complex sentences from the onlooker's point of view, bearing in mind first person, appropriate language and connectives.
- Share and discuss some of the sentences and select two or three for scribing.

Independent Writing
- Children finish rewriting the episode from the same point of view.
- Rewrite the episode in the first person from Tom's point of view.

Checking Children's Learning
- Can the children tell you what they had to change in order to write the same story from a different point of view?
- Have the children used complex sentences, with at least one subordinate clause?
- Can the children tell you, and demonstrate, two ways of connecting clauses in a complex sentence?

Revisiting the Objective
- Write the next episode from the dame's point of view.

Term 1 Unit of work 2:

Write a modern retelling

Writing objective

T6: To manipulate narrative perspective by producing a modern retelling.

Links to sentence/word level work

S6: To secure knowledge and understanding of more sophisticated punctuation marks.

Text Copymasters: C4–8

Discussing the Text

- Recap the episode together, discussing the sequence of events and what was said.
- Tell the children that this time you are going to write a modern retelling of this part of 'The Water Babies'.
- Discuss (1) what will *not* change: a poor, hungry and thirsty central character arriving at a place where he or she is given food and drink and relates his/her adventures.; (2) what *will* need to be changed to bring the story up to date: events leading up to the situation, the setting, the characters, the language.
- Decide (a) the situation, e.g. a runaway from home or children's home or (as in the Shared Writing Example, opposite) a street child in another country and (b) the gender and name of the central character.

Shared Writing

Teacher demonstration

- Quickly plan the episode. (1) The appearance of the central character and others' reactions; (2) The character asks for help; (3) He tells his story.
- Demonstrate writing the first sentence. As you write, comment on how you are writing e.g. adding detail by choosing adjectives (*I'll have him knocking on the door. What sort of knock would it be? Soft? Weak? Feeble?* – see Shared Writing Example) and expanding the sentence by dropping in a subordinate clause ('as it opened') and explaining the punctuation.
- Write the second sentence, demonstrating the use of a colon before a clause explaining the main clause.
- Re-read the first, complex, sentence of the original text. Write the third sentence about the reaction of those who see the main character for the first time. Commentate on the punctuation you use to expand the sentence with explanatory detail (see Shared Writing Example).

Teacher scribing

- Re-read the next few sentences. Scribe the conversation between the adult and the child, e.g. *What shall we call the schoolmaster? What do you think he says to Emilio? We need to write it in modern speech. How shall we write the reply?* etc.
- Scribe a complex sentence about the adult, explaining why he/she is cross. Include some more sophisticated punctuation marks (see suggestion under the Shared Writing Example).

Shared Writing Example

It all began with a feeble knock on the schoolroom door followed by, as the door swung open, the sight of a filthy, bedraggled figure lit by the bright sunshine behind. His clothes were torn and ragged: he had been living rough for so long. The children (girls and boys of between five and nine) giggled and nudged each other at this weird sight; but, after all that had happened to him, Emilio was too tired to care.

Signor Lopes, the class 4 teacher, was a gentle but firm man who hated being interrupted; he was, therefore, extremely exasperated when Emilio knocked on the door – this was the third interruption in half an hour – and, consequently, spoke sharply to the pathetic figure in front of him.

Supported composition
- Ask the children, in pairs, to write a complex sentence, using one or more of the kinds of punctuation you have been demonstrating, about the main character 'fainting'.
- Share results, select and scribe, discussing use of punctuation and possible alternatives. Expand and improve the sentence together, if desired.
- Ask the children to write a complex sentence about what the adult does next.
- Share, select and scribe, as above.

Independent Writing
- Children write the third part of the story. It should include dialogue and at least two complex sentences containing examples of: colon, semi-colon, dashes, brackets, and commas to denote parenthesis.

Checking Children's Learning
- Can the children tell you the key features of a modern retelling of an older story?
- Does the children's writing contain these elements?
- Can the children write a complex sentence containing one or more of the punctuation marks demonstrated in this session?

Revisiting the Objective
- Change the characters and setting to write a different retelling of this episode.

Term 1 Unit of work 3:

Write as a playscript

Writing objective

T9: To prepare a short section of story as a script, e.g. using stage directions, location/setting.

Text Copymasters: C4–7

Discussing the Text

- Tell the children that you are going to write the 'Chimney-sweep' episode as a playscript.
- Elicit children's existing knowledge of playscripts.
- Go through the text distinguishing between narrative, direct speech and reporting clauses. On the acetate sheet, you could annotate the text, using the code N, DS and RC; alternatively, you may wish to highlight the text in three colours. Identify where speech will need to be added.

Shared Writing

Teacher demonstration

- Write the title 'Chimney-sweep!' and the heading 'Cast List'. *Cast lists are often written in the order in which the characters appear, or with the main characters first.* List the names vertically. *We need to add who they are* (See Shared Writing Example).
- *Next, I need to write the setting.* Write 'Scene: The school room in the dame's cottage.'
- *How does the scene begin?* Look at the first paragraph. *What happens first? The children see Tom, so I will put a stage direction for the actor playing Tom, 'Enter Tom'. I think I will add a bit more to say how he enters and what he looks like.* Add 'in rags and tatters, staggering'.
- *Now I have to indicate that the girls cry and the boys laugh at Tom. I will write a stage direction for the girls: 'The girls see Tom and begin to cry'. I will add some dialogue between two boys.* Write the speeches for two boys (see Example), commenting on layout, spacing and lack of speech marks.
- *Now we come to the dame's first speech.* Talk about the need to make the language accessible for a modern audience and demonstrate with this speech. Write as in the Shared Writing Example.
- Continue with the rest of the speeches in the Shared Writing Example, pointing out:
  - that you are retaining the dialect
  - how to show how characters are speaking
  - how to show stage directions.

Teacher scribing

- Read the last sentence on Resource Book page 3. Ask children in pairs to discuss and write the stage directions and speech for the dame.
- Take suggestions, discuss, agree and scribe. Scribe Tom's speech.
- Read Resource Book page 4. Scribe the dame's speech and the stage directions, taking suggestions from the children. Remind them about brackets, present tense and note-form for stage directions, e.g. 'Exits and returns with cup and piece of bread'.

Chimney-sweep!

Cast

Tom, a poor chimney-sweep's boy

Dame, a school teacher

School boys and girls

Scene: The school room in the dame's cottage

Enter Tom, in rags and tatters, staggering.

The girls see Tom and begin to cry.

BOY 1 *(nudging his neighbour)*: Ooh, look at that! What a scarecrow! *(Laughs)*

BOY 2 *(pointing)*: Look, everybody, look at him!

DAME: What are you and what do you want? A chimney-sweep! Get away with you! I'll have no sweeps here.

TOM *(nearly fainting)*: Water!

DAME *(sharply)*: Water? There's plenty i' the beck.

TOM: But I can't get there; I'm faint with hunger and thirst. *(Sinks down on to the doorstep, leaning his head against the door post.)*

Supported composition

- Read the first sentence on page 5. Ask children in pairs to rewrite this as stage directions for Tom. Share efforts, select and add to playscript.
- Ask children to write the next two speeches, including any necessary directions. Share, select and scribe.

Independent Writing

- Children complete the playscript, including expanding 'he told all the truth in a few words' into a speech by Tom.

Checking Children's Learning

- Can the children describe the layout and features of a playscript?
- Are the children's playscripts laid out correctly?
- Can the children write stage directions clearly and concisely in the correct tense?

Revisiting the Objective

- Write what happens to Tom next as another scene in playscript form.

Writing objective

T7: To plan quickly and effectively the plot, characters and structure of their own narrative writing.

Links to sentence/word level work

S2: To transform a sentence from active to passive, and vice versa.

Text Copymasters: C8–9

Discussing the Text

- Explain to the children that they are going to read a story plan featuring a girl who has a problem because she has not done her homework.
- Read the plan on Resource Book pages 8 and 9.
- *There are two alternative endings, which one would you choose? Why?*
- *Does the ending you choose affect whether or not the girl seems to have learned anything from her experience?*
- *Can you think of an alternative ending?*
- *How would you describe the type of story this seems to be? Would it be a humorous one, for example? Is it a fantasy story or a realistic one?*

Shared Writing

Teacher demonstration

- Tell the children that you are going to give them the 'Ten-Question Guide' to planning a story and that they are going to use it to plan a story of their own.
- Write the ten questions in the Shared Writing Example. You may like to do this on a large sheet of card which can then be displayed in the room for future reference.
- Read and discuss the questions, making sure, for example, that children understand what is meant by 'initiating event'.

Teacher scribing

- Explain that you want to adapt the outline on pages 8 and 9 of the Resource Book to plan a different story about a child who has not done his/her homework. *For example, we could have a boy playing truant because he doesn't want to face his teacher and he meets a super intelligent alien who helps him with his homework.*
- Ask for suggestions as to a broad plot outline and reach consensus.
- Clip the acetate to page 8 of the Resource Book.
- Go through the first three headings making changes in line with your agreed plot outline. Tell the children they can always add extra characters later on if necessary.

Shared Writing Example

Planning a Story: the Ten-Question Guide

1. What type of story will it be?
2. Who is going to be in the story?
3. What is the setting? (Time and place)
4. Will it change?
5. Who is telling the story?
6. How does the story open?
7. What is the initiating event?
8. What happens as a result?
9. How is the situation resolved?
10. How will the story end?

Supported composition
- Ask the children to write down what should be in the opening.
- Take suggestions, select and scribe: *Do we want to leave 'feeling very worried'?*
- Repeat for the initiating event.
- Do not write anything down for the rest of the headings, simply take suggestions and discuss children's ideas.

Independent Writing
- Give out copies of Copymaster C1. Tell children that they have *five minutes only* to use the 'Ten-Question Guide' to planning a story to write up their own plan of the story developed in the Shared Writing.
- Give the children the title 'Late Again!' Explain that this time they have ten minutes to plan a story which fits the title. They should use your written list of the ten questions to guide them, i.e. not another copymaster.

Checking Children's Learning
- Share some of the plans.
- Were the children able to complete their planning in the allotted time?
- What did they find to be the easiest and most difficult aspects of the task?
- How helpful did they find the ten questions?

Revisiting the Objective
- Ask for suggestions for a snappy title. Choose one and plan the story together using the ten questions to guide the planning.

Note: Keep the Shared Writing for further work in Unit 5.

Term 1 Unit of work 5:

Write the story with two narrators

Writing objective

T6: To manipulate narrative perspective by writing a story with two different narrators.

Text Copymasters: C8–9

Discussing the Text

- Remind the children about the story outline from Unit 4 – re-reading it if necessary (see Resource Book pages 8 and 9).
- Tell them that they are going to write this short story but that they are going to do it from the point of view of two different characters – *in other words, two different narrators.*
- *The whole story will be written in the first person: the girl will tell the story as far as the wizard making suggestions for excuses to tell her teacher and then the dog will take over the story.*

Shared Writing

Session 1
Teacher demonstration

- *Our first paragraph needs to have the girl on her way to school and we need to say what the problem is. We could start like this:* write Shared Writing Example 1, opposite.
- Ask children to read your opening. Are they happy with it? *Is there anything you think we should change?*

Teacher scribing

- *I need to say that the girl hasn't done her homework so how should I continue? Should I say something about her dreading the moment when her teacher asks for her work?*
- Take suggestions, select and scribe to complete the paragraph.

Supported composition

- *Our next section needs to introduce the wizard and his dog and how the girl tells him about her problem.*
- Ask the children to write one or two sentences to introduce the wizard. Use Shared Writing Example 2 if they appear to need help.
- Take suggestions, select and scribe.
- Ask the children to write two or three sentences in which the girl explains her problem, then take suggestions, select and scribe.
- Read what has been written so far. *Are you happy with what we've done so far? Is there anything you think we should change?*

Teacher demonstration

- Refer to the story outline again. Explain that having written the opening and initiating event, you are going to leave the next section for children to write by themselves.
- *What I want us to do now is to think about how we can make the change to the second narrator, the dog.*

- *The wizard has been making suggestions for excuses so I'm going to write a very short paragraph to lead in to the change over …* See Shared Writing Example 3.
- *As I write the next part I want you to think about how I've made it obvious that we have a change in the narrator and what I'm showing about the character of the dog.* Write Shared Writing Example 4.
- Discuss children's responses. Draw out, for example, the dog's attitude to the wizard and the inference that it is the dog (who has been very much a secondary character until this point) who leads the wizard and is the more intelligent of the two.

Shared Writing Example

1. It usually takes me about three minutes to walk to school. Sometimes I run and get there faster but that morning I was like a snail.

2. I was startled by a voice coming from behind me. 'Good morning! And what a wonderful morning it is too – it makes an old wizard like me glad to be alive!'

3. The wizard was interrupted by a loud bark from his dog which made me look down. The funny little thing was staring at the wizard just as if he was trying to tell him something …

4. Of course I was trying to tell him something! I'd been sitting there for ages listening to all this nonsense – well, except when I wandered over to the lamp-post to investigate a rather nice smell. It was obvious what he had to do but, as always, it needed me to tell him.

Independent Writing
Session 2
- Children should be given 45 minutes of the literacy hour for independent writing in which they write the story. They can incorporate the sections from the shared writing if they wish and will also need to have pages 8 and 9 of the Resource Book on view.

Checking Children's Learning
- Share some of the stories or sections of children's writing.
- *How does having two narrators strengthen the story?*
- *Can we tell the difference between the two voices?*
- *Having written the story in this way, can you think of any other ways you could have used two narrators?*

Revisiting the Objective
- Brainstorm and list ways of writing dual-narrator stories, e.g. alternating chapters, a dialogue between two narrators.

Writing objective

T8: To summarise a passage, chapter or text in a specified number of words.

Links to sentence/word level work

S5: To form complex sentences, e.g. using different connecting devices …
exploring how meaning is affected by the sequence and structure of clauses.

Text Copymasters: C10–13

Discussing the Text

- Tell the children that the extract 'Oberon's Magic' is from Shakespeare's play
  'A Midsummer Night's Dream'. Read the text in the box at the top of Resource
  Book page 10. *What does this tell us?* Take responses. *It is a summary of
  what has just happened. In 48 words, it tells us the main things that have
  happened in the scene so far. In what tense is it written?* Examine the use
  of commas and brackets.
- *In this session, we are going to practise writing summaries.*
- Read from Snout's speech (page 10) to 'BOTTOM sings' (page 12). Look at
  the picture on page 11.

Shared Writing

Teacher demonstration

- *I will write a summary of this part of the play in no more than 30 words.
  What happens on page 10?* Take responses, e.g. 'Snout and Quince run off.'
  'Bottom has got a donkey's head. Turn these into a sentence (see Shared
  Writing Example, Summary 1). Count the number of words. Show how you
  might cut them down further, e.g. by changing 'when they see …' to 'on
  seeing …'
- Demonstrate how the order of clauses can be changed, e.g.
  'On seeing Bottom with a donkey's head, Snout and Quince run away'.
  'Snout and Quince run away, on seeing Bottom with a donkey's head.'
  Discuss whether this affects the meaning.
- Summarise the top half of page 12. Take oral summaries from the children
  then show how you would write this in one sentence (See Shared Writing
  Example, Summary 1). Explain your use of comma and brackets.

Teacher scribing

- Read Titania's first speech (page 12). *What has happened now? How can we
  write that as a sentence in no more than 15 words? Should we make it
  clear who Titania is/Have we got enough words spare?* (See Example,
  Summary 2)
- Read the next summary in the box (page 13). Look at the use of dashes instead
  of brackets. *Could we use dashes instead of brackets for 'Titania – the
  Queen of the fairies – '?* Try it and discuss the effect.

Shared Writing Example

Summary 1 (pages 10–12):

On seeing Bottom with a donkey's head, Snout and Quince run away. Bottom thinks his friends want to scare him, so he sings (to show them he is not afraid).

Summary 2 (page 12):

Bottom's singing wakes Titania, the Queen of the fairies, who falls in love with him.

Summary 3 (pages 13–14):

Titania tells her four fairies to be kind and polite to the donkey; to serve him in many ways: fetch him food, give him light and wake him gently.

Supported composition

- Read Titania's second speech (pages 13–14). Give children a minute's 'time out' to summarise in pairs what Titania tells her fairies to do.
- Write 'Titania tells her fairies to …' on the board and ask children to finish the sentence, summarising her speech. It should be a complex sentence. *Think about the punctuation you use between the clauses.* They may wish to write the summary in two sentences. They should use between 25 and 30 words.
- Share summaries. Select one. Scribe it and discuss punctuation. If you have time, change the order of clauses and discuss the effect on meaning.

Independent Writing

- Summarise the episode from 'The Water Babies' in 35 words.

Checking Children's Learning

- Can the children tell you what a summary is?
- Are their summaries clear, correctly punctuated and do they contain only the most important information?
- Can the children demonstrate how clauses could be changed round in a sentence?
- Can the children write a sentence containing two different connective devices?

Revisiting the Objective

- Put the summaries written for this unit of work together with the two summaries in the text (in the correct order). Write a summary of these summaries in 15 words!

Writing objective

T10: To write own poem experimenting with active verbs and personification; produce revised poems for reading aloud individually.

Links to sentence/word level work

S2: To revise earlier work on verbs and to understand the terms *active* and *passive*.

Text Copymaster: C14

Discussing the Text

- Ask the children to listen while you read the poem 'Death of a Snowman' (Resource Book page 16).
- *What do you think of the poem?*
- *Did the snowman really have fur on his hat?*
- *How well does the photograph fit the poem?*
- *What technique does the poet use to make us think of a melting snowman in a different way?* (personification)
- Explain or remind the children about the meaning of personification, e.g. *Personification is a form of metaphor where a writer or poet describes a non-human thing as if it were human.*
- Identify examples of the passive voice.

Shared Writing

Teacher demonstration

- Tell the children that they are going to write a poem called 'Houses' which uses personification. *It's going to be about an imaginary street with several different kinds of houses and there'll be one verse for each house.*
- *I'm going to start us off with the first verse which is about a bungalow, built around 80 years ago, surrounded with a border of flowers.* Write Shared Writing Example 1.
- Read the verse. *What do you think her eyes and her beads are?*
- *Let's see what other houses we could have.* Write Shared Writing Example 2 on a separate sheet of paper, leaving room for notes for each one.

Teacher scribing

- *We're going to turn each of these houses into people, just like I did with the bungalow at number 5. Who do you think number 7 could be?*
- Scribe notes of the children's suggestions, e.g. a rich man looking down on his neighbours, toys about him (cars in drive) puffing cigar (chimney)
- Repeat for the other three houses. (The recently built semi-detached houses could be young twins; number 13, a sad young woman wearing her unluckiness around her neck; number 15, a Sleeping Beauty waiting for someone to wake her or a neglected old tramp.)

Supported composition
- Split the class in half and allocate two houses to each half. Ask children, in pairs, to write phrases or lines for 'their' houses.
- Tell children that they will need to listen carefully to each other's suggestions. Ask as many pairs as possible to read out what they have done.
- Tell children to clean off their whiteboards.
- Split the class in half again. Ask the children, in pairs, to draft a verse for each of the two houses they did *not* write phrases or lines for.
- Ask as many pairs as possible to read out the verses they have written.
- Tell the children to clean off their whiteboards.

Independent Writing
Session 1
- Children draft their own 'Houses' poem. It should start with number 7 in the street and finish with number 17, i.e. a house they choose for themselves.

Session 2
- They should go through their poems, revise them and make a fair copy for display.
- The children should then take turns to read their poems to the group.

Checking Children's Learning
- Display the poems and select some to be read aloud to the class by the writer.
- Does the writer really make us see each of the houses in the street as people?

Revisiting the Objective
- Shared Writing: Write a 'Weather' personification poem with verses on wind, rain, thunder etc. as different people.
- Independent Writing: Write a 'Feelings' poem with verses on anger, jealousy etc as different people wearing different coloured clothes.

Write the next episode

Writing objective

T10: To use different genres as models to write, e.g. short extracts, sequels …
using appropriate conventions, language.

Links to sentence/word level work

S1: To identify examples of active and passive verbs in texts.

Text Copymasters: C15–18

Discussing the Text

- Tell the children that they are going to read an extract from a novel called 'The Turbulent Term of Tyke Tyler' by Gene Kemp. If children have read the book they will know that Tyke is a girl. If not, and they are likely to read it, try and avoid telling them because it will spoil things for them.
- Read the extract 'Bones' (Resource Book pages 18–21).
- Explain that a leat is a stream which carries water to a mill.
- Who is telling the story?
- *Can we infer anything about Tyke and Danny from this extract?*
- *How does the author show that Danny is excited in his first speech?*
- Points to notice and discuss about the author's style include: first person narrative; use of both past and present tense in the narrative; no use of reporting clauses ('said so and so'); examples of highly complex and extremely simple sentences; non-standard English for Danny's speech; asides from the narrator, e.g. at the top of Resource Book page 19.
- Re-read the final paragraph of the extract (page 21). What do children think that the bones will turn out to be?

Shared Writing

Teacher scribing

- Explain to children that they are going to plan and then write the next section of the story. *It is important to try and use a similar style to Gene Kemp so we are going to start by drawing up a style guide to help you.*
- Write the heading 'Style Guide' and first bullet point of Shared Writing Example 1. *The first thing we can say is that because it is an adventure story, it moves at quite a fast pace.*
- Ask the children to cast their minds back to the earlier discussion about the author's style and to suggest other things which you can list.
- Scribe children's suggestions, prompting where necessary, using Shared Writing Example 1 to help.
- Read the list through and display for children to refer to when they are writing independently.

Teacher demonstration

- Explain to children that you are going to write a list of questions which will help them plan what they are going to write. Tell them to be thinking about what they will decide for their own stories as you write.
- Write Shared Writing Example 2. Pause for discussion after the first question: the bones could turn out to be, for example, animal remains or a plastic model of a skeleton.

Shared Writing Examples

1. Style Guide

- adventure story so fast moving
- first person narrative (Tyke)
- mixture of past and present tense
- little or no use of reporting clauses in dialogue ('said so and so')
- a mixture of complex and simple sentence structure (complex for narrative, simple for dialogue?)
- non-standard English for Danny's speech
- asides from the narrator

2. Planning questions

- What is going to be the outcome – what have you decided about the bones?
- Do the children go past anything else before they reach the bones?
- What does Danny say when they get there?
- What does Tyke see and think at first?
- What do the children do next?

Supported writing

- Give the children a few minutes to jot down their responses to the planning questions.

Independent Writing

- Using the Style Guide, the planning questions and their own brief notes, the children should write the next episode. Give them a set amount of time in which to write.

Checking Children's Learning

- *Go through your writing. Would you say that you have included all the features in the Style Guide?*
- *Does your writing cover all the planning questions? Did you find them helpful to you?*
- Share some of the stories and discuss the above two points.

Revisiting the Objective

- Plan an adventure story about another strange find in an empty house.

Term 2 Unit of work 9:

Write a story using flashbacks

Writing objective

T11: To write own story using e.g. flashbacks or a story within a story to convey the passing of time.

Text Copymasters: C19–20

Discussing the Text

- Introduce the text 'A Flashback Story' (page 22) and explain that it is about writing a story which includes a flashback to the past. *Why do you think authors use flashbacks in story writing?*
- Tell the children that they will be writing stories based on this outline. Read the plot outline and say that you will come back to what the boy might have done.
- Read the opening.
- *What do you think of this as a story opening? Is it an effective one? Why?*

Shared Writing

Teacher scribing

- Tell the children that they have about a minute to discuss in pairs what they think the boy might have done wrong.
- Clip the acetate over page 22 of the Resource Book.
- Ask for children's ideas and scribe them as bullet points. See Shared Writing Example 1 (opposite) for suggestions.
- Discuss the ideas, for example: would some make a stronger story than others? Would some be easier than others for the boy to put right?

Supported composition

- Ask the children to write down, developing or adapting if necessary, the idea they will choose to write about. They should also write down the name they have chosen for the boy and what he will decide to do about what has happened.
- While they are writing, clean off the acetate and clip it over page 23.

Teacher demonstration

- Explain that the opening paragraph could be extended a little to improve the link into the flashback.
- Write Shared Writing Example 2. *I'm adding a little more about the boy and then leading into the flashback by using ellipsis. Dialogue is always a good way to start a flashback, so if you were having the event taking place in school you could have something like this …*
- Read the opening and what you have written. *You could also start the flashback by contrasting that day with the wet and miserable one of the opening.*
- *When you do your own story, you also need to think about how you will come back into the present. You could choose to do it like this, for example … Write Shared Writing Example 3. This leads into what the boy will decide.*
- *When you write your story you could make it a short story by simply telling your readers what his decision will be, or you could extend it by writing another episode which **shows** your readers what the decision was rather than telling them immediately.*

Shared Writing Example

1. What the boy might have done:

- been part of a bullying episode
- taken some money from his mother's purse
- allowed someone else to take the blame for something he broke or damaged either at home or school.
- torn up his school report because he thought it was a bad one
- been persuaded by a friend to shoplift
- written an unpleasant anonymous letter to an elderly neighbour

2. Leading into the flashback

His body was still but his mind was whirling as Friday forced its way back into his memory. It had started out like any other day …

'The bell will be going soon,' Miss Rogers said to her class.

3. Coming back to the present

The sound of his mother calling 'Are you awake yet?' dragged [*Boy's Name*] back to the present. He took a deep breath and, in that moment, he made his decision.

Independent Writing

- Children write their flashback stories. They can either copy the opening in the Resource Book and use the links from the Shared Writing Examples or compose a new ones.
- As a group, children share and comment on each other's stories. Revise the writing if and where necessary.

Checking Children's Learning

- How successfully have the children handled the links into and out of the flashback?
- *Do you think that your story would have worked as well if you had told it as a straight narrative rather than with a flashback?*

Revisiting the Objective

- Plan a similar story with two or more flashbacks, i.e. with interruptions to the flashback narrative by returns to the present.

Writing objective

T12: To study in depth one genre and produce an extended piece of similar writing ... to revise, redraft this and bring to presentational standard ...

Links to sentence/word level work

S3: To revise work on complex sentences ... constructing complex sentences; appropriate use of punctuation.

Text Copymasters: C21–22

Discussing the Text

- Have the acetate clipped to Resource Book page 24, 'Revising Your Writing'.
- Explain to the children that they are going to read some advice on revising their writing.
- Read through the text on story structure.
- *What could we say here instead of 'telling the story?'* (the narrator) Annotate the question in the text.
- *It says here 'What starts everything off?' What phrase would we often use instead?* (Initiating Event) Annotate.
- *It says 'What happens because of this?' What do we call this part of a story?* (e.g. the Action–Reaction pattern) Annotate accordingly.
- *What is the word we often use to describe the 'high point of the action'?* (Climax) Write the word.
- *What could we use instead of 'How is the problem ...'?* (Resolution).

Shared Writing

Session 1
Supported composition

- Ask the children to read the text through silently and think for a moment if there is anything else they would want to add to the list. Remind them that it is only to do with the structure of the story.
- Discuss this in pairs and write down any additional questions they can think of. *For example, would you want to add anything about flashbacks or dialogue?*

Teacher scribing

- Take the children's suggestions and scribe the appropriate ones.
- Add anything which you think should be included (See Shared Writing Example 1.)

Independent Writing

- The children should use Copymaster C21 to copy your annotations and additions for later use.

Discussing the Text

Session 2

- Have the acetate clipped to page 25 of the Resource Book.
- Read through the text on style.
- Ask the children if there is anything which they don't quite understand or need to have clarified.

Supported composition

- Ask the children to read the text through silently and think for a moment if there is anything else they would want to add to the list.
- Discuss this in pairs and write down any additional questions they can think of. For example, would you want to add anything about complex sentences or Standard English?

Teacher scribing

- Take the children's suggestions and scribe the appropriate ones.
- Add anything which you think should be included (See Shared Writing Example 2.)
- Give children Copymaster C22 to copy down the additional questions.

Shared Writing Example

1. Story Structure

- Could you improve the story by changing part of it to a flashback?
- Have you included sufficient dialogue?
- Have you included any characters which are not really necessary?
- Will the reader be clear as to what is happening, when and why?

2. Style

- Are there simple sentences which could be improved by making them into complex sentences?
- Have you written anything which is non-Standard English – unless it is deliberate?
- Can you show how characters are feeling rather than simply telling the reader?

Independent Writing

- The children should select a story they have recently written. They should then work in pairs to go through and mark up each story using their annotated Copymasters C21 and 22. The writer of the story has the final word on suggested changes/revisions.

Checking Children's Learning

- *How did the guidance help in looking for possible revisions to your work?*

Revisiting the Objective

- As a class, use the guidance to revise one volunteer's work.

Writing objective

T13: Parody a literary text, describing stock characters and plot structure, language etc.

Links to sentence/word level work

S3: To revise work on complex sentences … constructing complex sentences; appropriate use of punctuation.

Text Copymasters: C23–28

Discussing the Text

- Introduce the extract 'Captain Hook's Plan' and read together Resource Book pages 26 to 31.
- *Who has read 'Peter Pan'? Can you remember what came of the plan?*
- *How does Hook's mood change during the extract?*
- *What is the relationship between the two characters?*
- *What do you think of the illustrations of Captain Hook and Smee? Are they as you would imagine these characters to be?*
- Identify examples of complex sentences and their punctuation.
- Tell the children that they are going to write a *parody* of this type of story.
- Ensure that they understand the term 'parody', particularly its emphasis on humour.

Shared Writing

Teacher demonstration

- Explain that first of all you are going to look at some of the language features of the extract which could be used in the parody.
- Write Shared Writing Example 1, opposite, or have it already prepared. *These are some of the ways the author describes Hook and shows his mood …*
- Discuss the examples and moods and feelings they indicate.

Teacher scribing

- *Now let's list the words and sayings that the pirates use. 'We'll call this list Pirate Language'.*
- Go through the text for the children to identify the examples listed in Shared Writing Example 2.
- Ask children if they know any other sayings or expressions used by pirates and scribe their suggestions as in Shared Writing Example 3.

Supported composition

- Tell the children that they are going to write a short parody which features two pirates: *the evil Captain Thumb whose fingers were chewed off by a tortoise and who can't run very fast because she has two wooden legs, and Flea, one of her men.* They are hatching a plot to steal treasure from a character the children should create.
- Ask children to make brief character notes on each of the three characters they will be using.
- Share some of the children's ideas.

Shared Writing Example

1. Character and mood

- Hook barked petulantly
- there was a quiver in his voice
- he said huskily
- He laughed but in a hollow way.
- Hook wetted his dry lips
- a curdling smile lit up his swarthy face
- replied slowly through his teeth

2. Pirate Language

- Aye
- Odds bobs, hammer and tongs
- Unrip your plan
- a jolly thickness
- Aha
- it's the wickedest, prettiest policy ever I heard of

3. Other Pirate sayings

- Shiver me timbers
- Land ahoy!
- yo ho ho and a bottle of rum
- Walk the plank!
- me hearties
- splice the mainbrace
- hoist the Jolly Roger

Independent Writing

- Children write their short parody. They should try and use many of the expressions etc. listed in the Shared Writing.

Checking Children's Learning

- Share some of the children's writing.
- *How humorous are the parodies? What is it that makes them funny?*
- What language similarities are there with the extract from Peter Pan?

Revisiting the Objective

- Plan a parody of a Super Hero story – Batman? Superman?

Writing Objective

T14: To write commentaries or summaries crediting views expressed by using expressions such as 'The writer says that …'.

Text Copymasters: C29–30

Discussing the Text

- Introduce and read Ute Prayer to the children (Resource Book pages 32–33).
- *What do you think of this prayer?*
- *What do you think that 'as blossoms are humble with beginning' means?*
- *What does 'the fall' mean?*
- *Why does the writer only use examples from the natural world?* (because s/he is praying to the Earth and also because this is the environment in which s/he lives and therefore knows best.)
- *The prayer is described as 'Traditional' and is unlikely to have been written down originally, so how has it survived and reached you today?*

Teacher scribing

- Tell the children that they are going to comment on the poem in writing – in other words, write a commentary.
- Ask the children to suggest things they might comment on: *For example, should you give a summary of what the person is praying for?*
- Scribe their suggestions and prompt and scribe to include those in Shared Writing Example 1.

Shared Writing

Teacher demonstration

- Tell the children that you are going to give them an example of the way a commentary can be written. *I'm going to show you how I would write the part about the origins of the prayer.*
- Write Shared Writing Example 2, commenting as you write on word choices, sentence structure and punctuation. (For example, words and phrases signalling speculation.) Point out that you are using an impersonal style of writing and avoiding saying things like 'I think …'
- Read it aloud.
- *Can you find an example of where I have speculated and stated an opinion and then justified it?*

Supported composition

- Ask the children to write the section about the use of examples from the natural world.
- Take examples and discuss. Has anyone included quotes from the prayer?

Shared Writing Example

1. Things to comment on

- written in the first person and seems like a very personal prayer
- summary of what the person is praying for
- the form of the prayer
- the writer only uses examples from the natural world – why?
- the use of imagery (e.g. blossoms, fields)
- what you think of the examples and images
- probably not written down originally, so an English translation
- might the prayer have been used at a particular time? (at a ceremony to mark passing from boyhood to manhood?)
- might there be similar prayers in other tribes?

2. Commentary example

There is no one person named as the writer of this prayer – we only know that it is a traditional prayer from the Ute tribe of North America. Since it would not have been written down originally, it seems likely that it would have been handed down by word of mouth until someone, somewhere, translated it into English and wrote it down.

It is possible that the prayer was used at a particular time – for example, at a ceremony to mark the passing from boyhood to manhood. This seems reasonable because all the qualities that are prayed for are virtues which an adult would hope to possess.

Independent Writing

- Leave the prayer and 'Things to comment on' list on view for children to write their own commentaries. Remind them to justify their opinions and refer to the prayer where they can.
- Work with a partner, read each other's work and check that you have included all the necessary points from the list.

Checking Children's Learning

- Have children justified their opinions and referred to the prayer where they can?
- How have children signalled speculation?
- Are there clear distinctions between fact, speculation and opinion?
- Have children used complex sentence structures?

Revisiting the Objective

- Ask children to vote for an extract in the Resource Book which you can use to write a class commentary.

Writing objective
T7: To annotate passages in detail in response to specific questions.

Text Copymasters: C31–35

Discussing the Text

- Tell the children that you are going to make notes on 'Meeting', which is an extract from 'Goodnight Mr Tom', in order to write a character sketch of Tom.
- Read the text on Resource Book pages 34 to 39. *What does the text tell us about Tom?*

Shared Writing

Teacher demonstration

- Have ready the acetate sheet and pen.
- Tell the children that you are going to show them one way of making notes on a text. *I am going to re-read the text, paragraph by paragraph. When I reach a part which I think answers the question "What does the text tell us about Tom?", I am going to **annotate** the text: I will make notes in the margin to explain what I think the text tells us.*
- Read the first paragraph aloud. Underline 'bluntly' and Tom's speech. *He says "Yes. What do you want?", bluntly. What does that tell me? He's a blunt person, not very polite; so I will write that in the margin.* Write 'blunt, impolite' in the margin.
- Continue in this way, repeating the question, verbalising your thought processes and demonstrating underlining and annotation on pages 34 and 35. (See Shared Writing example)

Teacher scribing

- Continue reading and ask children to put up their hands when they think the text tells us something about Tom. Discuss and annotate at their suggestion.
- Stop at 'Near a church' (page 38, line 3).

Supported composition

- Ensure that pairs of children have Text Copymasters 31 to 35.
- Continue reading to 'It read "William Beech"' (final line of page 38).
- Ask children, in their pairs, to read to the end, asking themselves 'What does the text tell us about Tom?'. *Underline the parts about Tom. Make notes in the margin about what this tells us.*
- Discuss children's notes and annotate the final page. The penultimate paragraph gives a physical description of Tom for the first time. Have the children annotated Willie's view of what Tom looked like? Discuss. The last two sentences tell us more about his character.

Shared Writing Example

Suggested annotations

blunt   *impolite*

"Yes," said Tom bluntly, on opening the front door. "What d' you want?"

....

I'm the Billeting Officer for this area," she began.

                                                          He interrupts
"Oh yes, and what's that got to do wi' me?"   *rude, speaks sharply*

She flushed slightly. "Well, Mr, Mr ..."   *He makes her stammer*

"Oakley. Thomas Oakley."   *a man of few words*

....

"Mr. Oakley, with the declaration of war imminent ..."   *Interrupts again*

Impatient
Tom waved his hand. " I knows all that. Git to the point. What d' you want?" He

                                   dialect
noticed a small boy at her side.
                                   where does he come from?

Independent Writing

- On Text Copymasters 31 to 35 (all five text pages), children underline and write their own annotations in answer to the question 'What does the text tell us about Tom?'
- Write a character study of Tom, using the information from the annotated text.

Checking Children's Learning

- Can the children tell you what annotation is?
- Can the children explain how to annotate text?

Revisiting the Objective

- Annotate the text in the same way in answer to the question 'What does the text tell us about Willie?' in order to write a character study of Willie.

Writing objective

T8: To use a reading journal effectively to raise and refine personal responses to a text and prepare for discussion.

Text Copymasters: C31–35

Discussing the Text

- Children will need reading journals for this session.
- If children are not already keeping reading journals, the Shared Writing session will form a useful introduction. Discuss the use of reading journals generally and the range of possible contents:
- *One purpose for a reading journal is to write your feelings about what you are reading in preparation for a discussion with others. We are going to write an entry about the passage from 'Goodnight Mr Tom' when Tom and Willie meet.*
- Ask children to summarise the text orally.

Shared Writing

Teacher demonstration

- Have the text 'Meeting' displayed for reference.
- *There are three main characters in 'Meeting'. We will write our feelings about each one. If we have any questions or predictions about the character, we will write those as well. I will start by writing what I feel about the Billeting Officer at this point in the story.*
- *The text says that the Billeting Officer is harassed (page 34). I feel sympathetic towards her; having to look after all those children. I'll write something down about that.* (See Shared Writing Example)
- Read the parts of the text that refer to the Billeting Officer, comment on how she is doing her job conscientiously and write the rest of your personal response to her (see Shared Writing Example).
- *Have I got any questions I want to ask about her, if I was going to read on?*
- *No. I think she is a minor character who probably doesn't appear again.*

Teacher scribing

- *Now we'll write what we think and feel about Tom, as he is presented in this short extract.* Write the heading 'Tom'.
- Give children 30 seconds to write their thoughts and/or feelings in note form in their journals, e.g. 'a grumpy old man'. Take some responses. Discuss how they might be written in sentences, using an informal, personal style. Scribe, e.g. 'We think he might be grumpy because he is lonely.'
- If children respond with answers such as 'I don't like him', ask for reasons, take others' suggestions for elaborating on the original statement and scribe the expanded version.
- *In reading journals, it is useful to make a note of any questions that come up as we read. We can bear these in mind as we read further chapters. Have we got any questions we want to ask about Tom?* Take suggestions and scribe, e.g. *How do Tom and Willie get on? How will he treat Willie? Does he change?*

Meeting (from 'Goodnight Mr Tom' by Michelle Magorian)

What I think about the Billeting Officer

She is harassed because she has lots of children to look after. I feel sympathetic towards her, knowing what that is like. I feel even more sorry for her when Tom is rude and makes her nervous. She is only trying to do her job. She seems conscientious to me because she trying to do what the child's mother wants.

Supported composition

- Re-read the parts of the text that are about Willie.
- Ask the children to write their personal feelings about Willie in their journals, under the heading 'Willie'.
- Share and discuss clarity of expression. Select one sentence and scribe.

Independent Writing

- Children finish writing their personal responses to Willie and write questions they want to ask about him.
- In the reading journal, write a summary of the character study of Tom and/or Willie, written in previous sessions.

Checking Children's Learning

- Can the children tell what sort of things their reading journals might contain.
- Can the children write a thoughtful personal response to text read?
- Do the children support their opinions with evidence from the text, when writing in their journals?
- Can the children write appropriate and searching questions about text read?

Revisiting the Objective

- Use 'Chimney Sweep!', Unit 1 (Resource Book pages 2 to 6), to write an entry in the reading journal giving a personal response to Tom and the dame.

Term 3 Unit of work 15:

Compare texts in writing

Resource Book
pages 34–39
and 2–7

Writing objective

T12: To compare texts in writing, drawing out: their different styles and preoccupations; their strengths and weaknesses; their different values and appeal to a reader.

Links to sentence/word level work

S1: To revise the language conventions and grammatical features of the different types of text such as narrative …

Text Copymasters: C31–35 and C4–7

Discussing the Text

- Tell the children that you are going to compare 'Meeting' (pages 34 to 39) with 'Chimney-sweep!' (pages 2 to 6). Session 1 will involve making notes of the similarities and differences between the two. In session 2 the notes will be used to write a comparison of the two.
- Re-read both texts. *What kind of texts are they? Yes, narrative. How can you tell? What do we know about narratives?* Recap the usual structure of narratives and explain that both these texts are single events or episodes from longer novels.

Shared Writing

Session 1
Teacher demonstration

- In this session, make notes about each extract on an enlarged version of the table on Copymaster C2, 'Comparing texts'.
- Discuss the event in each text. *They are both about characters meeting for the first time so I will write 'A first meeting' in each of the first boxes.*
- Agree the main characters and demonstrate writing their names and a summary description of what they are (see Shared Writing Example opposite). *I will put the Billeting Officer in 'Meeting' in brackets as she is not a main character meeting for the first time, but she plays an important part in the event.*
- *What is the theme of each extract? Although one is about an evacuee and one is about a runaway chimney sweep, they are both about young boys in difficult situations, so I will write that* (see Shared Writing Example opposite).
- Now fill in one point about style and one point about language in column 1 for 'Chimney-sweep!'

Teacher scribing

- Discuss the style and language of 'Meeting', re-reading the text for evidence, and make notes in each box in column two, comparing with 'Chimney-sweep!' each time. Add further points in column one.
- Discuss the appeal of each text. *Who might each appeal to? Why do they appeal?* Scribe agreed notes.

Independent Writing

- Children complete the table on their own copies of Copymaster C2.

Comparing texts

C2

	Chimney-sweep!	Meeting
Event	A first meeting	A first meeting
Characters	Tom – a young chimney-sweep Dame – an old teacher	Tom – an old man Willie – a young evacuee (the Billeting Officer – a middle-aged woman)
Theme	Chimney-sweeps: a boy in problematic situation	Evacuees: a boy in a problematic situation
Style	Realistic dialogue uses questions, exclamations dialect, short sentences. Little description of the characters. Longer sentences with many 'ands'.	Realistic dialogue uses questions, short and long sentences. Characters described well.
Language	Old-fashioned, difficult to understand. Interesting, dialect words bring speech to life. Little use of adverbs, describing how characters speak. Few adjectives.	Modern, easy to understand. Some dialect. Adverbs tell how characters speak, e.g. bluntly, impatiently. Adjectives used to describe people, e.g. 'harassed middle-aged woman'
Appeal	Victorians – interesting? Makes the reader feel sorry for Tom. Involves you with the main character.	WW2 – interesting? Involves you with both characters. Makes you want to read on, find out what happens to Willie and Tom.

Shared Writing

Session 2

Teacher demonstration

- Display the completed table from Session 1 prominently.
- Quickly recap on the notes, making comparisons across the two columns.
- *How am I going to turn the notes into a piece of writing, comparing the two texts? I need to say something about what they are about, and how they are the same or different. Let's look at the event, characters and theme.* Write two or three sentences combining these notes, commenting on the use of a clause beginning with 'although' to make comparisons (See Shared Writing Example opposite).
- Write one or two sentences comparing the use of dialogue.

Teacher scribing

- Discuss character description in the two passages and write a paragraph comparing the two authors' writing.
- Continue writing from the notes on language, taking suggestions from the class.

Independent Writing

- Children write about the relative appeal of the two texts for children today, including their personal opinions, to be supported by reference to the texts.

Checking Children's Learning

- Can the children compare two texts orally?
- Can the children make comparisons of one or two features of two texts in writing, making reference to the text?

Revisiting the Objective

- Compare 'Captain Hook's Plan' with 'Bones', in the same way, using the table on Copymaster C3 to make notes before writing the comparison.

Shared Writing Example

Session 2

Both of these texts are about a young boy meeting an older person. Although the situations and times are very different – one is about a Victorian chimney sweep and one is about an evacuee during World War Two – both are about boys in difficulty, far away from home.

Both authors use a lot of dialogue and the characters speak in dialect, which brings it to life. The dialogue in 'Meeting' is easier to understand than the dialogue in 'Chimney-sweep!' because 'Chimney sweep!' was written over a hundred years ago.

Term 3 Unit of work 16:

Write a sequence of poems

Writing objective

T13: To write a sequence of poems linked by theme or form.

Text Copymasters: C36–37

Discussing the Text

- Introduce the poems and explain that there are three poems which are linked by both form and theme.
- Remind children that a cinquain is a poem with five lines and a total of 22 syllables. They are arranged in lines of 2, 4, 6, 8 and 2 syllables.
- Read the poems to the class.
- *Which one do you like most? Why?*
- *How does the poet convey the speed of the stream?* ('Rushing'; the use of short vowel sounds.)
- Comment on the differences with regard to light and the stage or part of the river as well as the time of day.

Shared Writing

Teacher demonstration

- Tell children that they are going to write a similar sequence of poems called 'Woodland Cinquains'; there will be four verses, one for each season and you have written the first one to start them off. Remind them of the 2, 4, 6, 8 and 2 syllables structure.
- Show Shared Writing Example 1.
- Ask children to read it aloud for you – while you listen attentively.
- *Hearing you read the poem aloud helped me and showed that there are a couple of changes I ought to make. The first one is that the syllable structure is wrong. Which line is not right? Yes, there are only 7 syllables in the fourth line so I'm going to change it to 'a hint of green' to get the extra syllable I need.* Make the change.
- I think there is too much alliteration in the second and third lines and 'brown branches' isn't very strong – it's also quite difficult to say. So I'm going to write this instead. Change as in Shared Writing Example 2.
- Read the revised poem.

Independent Writing

- Tell children that you want them to write the next three poems in the sequence: summer, autumn and winter. *Each of those words has got two syllables so there you are, I've done the first lines of each poem for you!* A third of the class should write the summer poem, a third autumn and a third the winter poem.
- While children are composing, write a fair copy of the spring poem plus the title. You will eventually end up with four sheets of paper which, when illustrated, will make a good corridor display.

Shared Writing

Teacher scribing

- Ask children to read aloud their summer cinquains. Discuss, select or vote on the one for you to scribe. Make any necessary amendments or amalgamations.
- Repeat for the autumn and winter cinquains.
- Read the whole sequence aloud – a final chance to make changes.

Shared Writing Examples

1. **Woodland Cinquains**

   The Spring

   Gives birth to buds

   Which burst from brown branches.

   Trees are showing hints of green:

   New life.

2. The Spring

   ~~Gives birth to buds~~ Calls out the buds

   Which burst from ~~brown~~ bare branches.

   Trees are showing ~~hints~~ a hint of green:

   New life.

Checking Children's Learning

- Can the children tell you the structure of a cinquain?
- Can they identify particularly effective word choices in their own and other children's poems?

Revisiting the Objective

- Write a series of poems entitled Sky Cinquains: the first is at sunrise, the second is about gathering rain clouds and storms, the third is about clear skies after the storm has gone and the fourth is at night.

Term 3 Unit of work 17:

Write a summary

Resource Book pages 42–47

Writing objective

T9: To write summaries of books or parts of books, deciding on priorities relevant to purpose.

Text Copymasters: C38–43

Discussing the Text

- Tell the children that you are going to read 'Reunion' and then write a summary of it for the review which you will be writing.
- Ask them to give you a definition of a summary. Remind the children about the summary you wrote of 'A Midsummer Night's Dream'. *What did we do then?*
- Read the first paragraph. *What is this? It's a summary of what has gone before. In 30 words it tells us the story* (a short novel) *of Lena and her family in the second world war.* This is the end of the story.
- Read the whole extract.

Shared Writing

Teacher demonstration

- *How can we reduce this exciting and moving ending to no more than 100 words, to give other people the essence of what it is about? We need to decide what is essential and which details are unimportant.*
- *First we need to tell the reader, as briefly as possible, who it is about and where they are.* Re-read paragraph one of the extract. Write a sentence of no more than 15 words about the family (See Shared Writing Example 1).
- *What important thing happens?* Scan the next paragraphs to the end of page 43, summarising orally, e.g. 'Snow falls, people seen in the distance, Lena hears a mouth-organ, it is her father, they hug.' Take the children's responses. Model a summary paragraph (See Shared Writing Example 1), commenting on what details you decide to leave out (e.g. the snow), what you regard as essential (mouth-organ? Father?) and the use of 'reunited' to summarise the whole event.

Teacher scribing

- Re-read page 45. *What is this part about? What is the significance of the stained glass angel?* Take suggestions for a summary sentence. Refine and scribe. (See Shared Writing Example 2)

Supported composition

- Read from the top of page 46 to '… somewhere, some day.' Ask children, in pairs to summarise how the father found his family. *Work it out orally first, then write it in one or two sentences, no more than 25 words in total.*
- Compare summaries. *Do they keep the important information? Can we cut out anything else, without destroying the meaning?* Select a summary, scribe and then re-draft together if necessary. (See Example 3.)

Shared Writing Example

1. Demonstration

Lena is in a concentration camp with her mother and sister but separated from her father.

Suddenly, she hears a mouth-organ in the distance. It is their father, They are joyfully reunited as a family.

2. Scribing

Their father shows them a little stained glass angel which he had kept all the time he was looking for them.

3. Supported Composition

He found them by playing his mouth-organ wherever he went. Children recognised him and told him about his daughters.

4. Independent Writing

They are homeless but together. It ends hopefully, with them looking forward to finding a new home.

Independent Writing

- Write a summary of the ending of the extract in about 20 words. (See Shared Writing Example 4.)

Checking Children's Learning

- Can children tell you what a summary is?
- Have children successfully summarised the last part of the extract in writing?

Revisiting the Objective

- Summarise 'Meeting' in approximately 100 words.

Writing objective

T11: To write a brief helpful review tailored for real audiences.

Links to sentence/word level work

S1: To revise the language conventions and grammatical features of the different types of text.

Text Copymasters: C38–43

Discussing the Text

- Discuss children's experience of writing book reviews, their purpose, audience and content. Compare with writing in a reading journal: both give you an opportunity to write your personal response to what you have read, but one is private, the other is public for other people.
- Tell children you are all going to write a short review of 'Reunion' for other children. Decide on the audience and method of publication, e.g. corridor display, school magazine, e-mail or website.

Shared Writing

Teacher demonstration

- *What shall we include in our reviews? What will be helpful for someone who has not read the story? I am going to write my paragraph headings to organise my thoughts.* Write some headings on the flipchart (see Shared Writing Example).

Supported composition

- Give children a short time to write these headings on whiteboards or in their reading journals.

Teacher demonstration

- Keeping the paragraph headings visible, start to write your review.
- *For my review, I am going to start by giving the title, author and by saying that this extract is from the end of a story.* Write sentence 1 (see Shared Writing Example).
- Re-read the shared summary written in the last session. (See Example 2.) Discuss whether anything needs to be added or deleted. Rewrite the summary for paragraph two, refining it as you go.
- *'My reactions to the text'* – tell children and write your response, e.g. example 3.

Supported composition

- Give children time to discuss each of the headings and make a brief note under each.
- Discuss one or two notes made under each heading. Draw out the difference between the factual summary of content and the expression of opinions. Remind children that they should back up their opinions of the author's language and style with examples in quotation marks. Model this.

Shared Writing Example

Paragraph Headings

- Title, author and genre
- Summary of the text
- My reactions to the text
- Character portrayal
- The author's style and language
- My message to the review reader

1. 'Reunion' is the end of the story 'The Angel with a Mouth-Organ' by Christabel Mattingley.

2. Lena is in a concentration camp with her mother and sister but separated from her father.

Suddenly, she hears a mouth-organ in the distance. It is their father, They are joyfully reunited as a family.

Their father shows them a little stained glass angel which he had kept all the time he was looking for them.

He found them by playing his mouth-organ wherever he went. Children recognised him and told him about his daughters.

They are homeless but together. It ends hopefully, with them looking forward to finding a new home.

3. It made me want to read the whole book straightaway because I felt involved with the characters who meet after such a long separation.

Independent Writing

- The children write their own reviews of 'Reunion', using the paragraph headings and notes to structure them.

Checking Children's Learning

- Can the children tell you the contents of a review?
- Can the children distinguish between facts and opinions in each others' reviews?
- Do the children know how to make a review helpful to a reader?
- Are the children's reviews clear, concise, personal and reasoned?

Revisiting the Objective

- Write a review of 'Captain Hook's Plan' (pages 26 to 31), using the same paragraph structure.

Term 3 Unit of work 19:

Write a back cover blurb

Resource Book pages 42–47

Writing objective

T10: To write a brief synopsis of a text, e.g. for back cover blurb.

Links to sentence/word level work

S4: To secure control of complex sentences.

Text Copymasters: C38–43

Discussing the Text

- Tell the children you are going to write a blurb for the back cover of 'The Angel with a Mouth-Organ'. *What is the purpose of blurbs?* Bring out the following: to engage someone who has picked up the book and tell them enough about it to persuade them to want to read it.
- *What should a blurb contain?* Focus on genre, setting and a synopsis of the story. Explain that a synopsis is a shortened summary.
- Turn to the first page of 'Reunion' and recap what you know about the book, re-reading the summary at the beginning if necessary.

Shared Writing

Teacher demonstration

- Discuss what you might put in this particular blurb. *I am going to note down what I want to include. Genre? A story. Setting? World War Two, Germany, concentration camps. Characters? Lena and her family, separated from their father. What else shall I include? The angel with a mouth-organ – that's intriguing. I think it will make the reader want to read the book.*
- Write the first sentence, talking as you write, e.g. *I could write 'This story is set in WW2, in German concentration camps. It is about Lena and her mother and sister who are separated from their father. Does that 'hook' the reader? It's not very interesting. I'll see if I can combine all that in one sentence.* Write a first draft of sentence 1 as a compound sentence. Demonstrate how to improve it by changing the three main clauses joined by 'and' to a complex sentence with subordinate clauses (see Shared Writing Examples 1 and 2). Discuss the punctuation needed.

Supported composition

- *How shall we write about the angel with the mouth-organ? One way might be in the form of questions to the reader.*
- Ask the children to discuss with a partner how they would write about it, and then write individually. See Shared Writing Example 3.
- Share efforts. If the children have written about how the story ends, use the opportunity to discuss whether this is appropriate for a blurb! Compare statements, if any, and questions. Discuss their effects. Choose one and scribe.

Teacher scribing

- Re-read the blurb together. Discuss the effect. *Does this meet the purpose of a blurb? Do we need to say anything else, e.g. Should we include a guide for who it is suitable for?* Scribe suggestions (See Example 4).

Shared Writing Example

1. Sentence 1, First Draft:

It is World War Two Germany (and) Lena ~~and~~ her mother and sister are
imprisoned together in a series of concentration camps, ~~and they do not~~ <ins>not knowing</ins>
~~know~~ what has happened to their father.

2. Sentence 1, Second Draft:

World War Two Germany – Lena, her mother and sister, are imprisoned
together in a series of concentration camps, not knowing what has
happened to their father.

3. Suggested Supported Composition

Who or what is the angel with the mouth-organ? What part does it play in the
story?

4. Suggested Teacher Scribing

An exciting read for ten to twelve year olds.

Independent Writing

- The children write a synopsis for a back cover blurb for 'Meeting', or for the whole novel 'Goodnight Mr Tom', if they have read it.

Checking Children's Learning

- Can the children tell you the purpose and features of a back cover blurb?
- Can the children write a brief synopsis that contains the essential elements of the text?

Revisiting the Objective

- For a class novel read recently or a book the children know well, write a synopsis for a back cover blurb, using a similar process to that given above.

Writing objective

T14: To write an extended story, worked on over time on a theme identified in reading.

Text Copymaster: C44

Discussing the Text

- Explain that today's session is about starting children off on a long story in chapters which they will be writing over a period of time.
- Tell them that they will be writing a fantasy story and that before you start to think about planning it, you want to examine the nature of fantasy stories.
- Either give out individual copies of Copymaster C3, 'Fantasy Stories', which children can keep for reference or make a copy of it for yourself for use on the overhead projector.
- Go through it with the children.
- Introduce the outline on page 48 of the Resource Book. Explain that you will use this to plan the first part of a story together and that children can either use this for their own stories or plan a completely different one.

Shared Writing

Teacher demonstration

- *The title of our story is 'Strange Meeting'. We've read two extracts about meetings in this book already but this time we are taking the idea of a meeting and making a fantasy story out of it.*
- Clip the acetate to the page. Tell the children that you are going to start an example chapter outline. *I'm going to start in the real world with an ordinary human character who has a problem.* Write Shared Writing Example 1.
- *In Chapter 2 Gavin meets someone, a woman.* Write Shared Writing Example 2.
- *Chapter 3 is where the fantasy, the 'unreal' starts …* Write Shared Writing Example 3.
- *The gist of the story is that the woman needs the help of a human to overcome a problem involving a struggle between good and evil. Gavin helps her and in the process grows in confidence and learns that he is not a coward which eventually will help him stand up to the bullies.*

Teacher scribing

- *What do you think could happen now that the crystal bubble has appeared?* Take suggestions from the children, select and scribe along the lines of Shared Writing Example 4.

Shared Writing Example

1. Real world setting: Gavin, 11 years old, small for his age, is being bullied – too frightened to stand up for himself. Start with episode of bullies taking something from him and destroying it.

2. Gavin sitting in corner of park, crying. Woman asks what is the matter. Gavin explains, says he's a coward. Woman says she has problem too – they can help each other.

3. She takes off crystal earring, puts it on ground. It grows into huge crystal bubble.

4. They get into bubble which spins and rises – what Gavin sees on journey to another world. Woman explains her problem.

5. They arrive and get out of bubble. What does Gavin see? Where will the woman take him? What happens?

Supported composition
- *We need to have the woman explaining who she is and what her problem is before they arrive. Work in pairs to discuss and then make notes on who she could be and the problem she has.*
- Discuss what the children have written for the rest of Chapter 3.
- Write Shared Writing Example 5 in the space for Chapter 4.

Independent Writing
- The children work in pairs or individually to write their own chapter plans for the complete story. They can either use what you have done together or adapt it, (e.g. have a girl as the main character) or they can write a completely new version. They could write on paper or use Copymaster C44, continuing on the reverse of the sheet. Stress that they should be writing an outline only, i.e. not too much detail.
- Discuss the chapter plans in groups to give feedback to individual children and their plans.
- Write the story over a period of time. Have discussion and feedback group sessions from time to time where children review what they have done, where they are going and if the chapter plan needs to be adapted.

Checking Children's Learning
- For the children who are following the shared scenario, do they include something about Gavin dealing with the bullies at the end?
- Can the children describe what makes a fantasy story?

Revisiting the Objective
- For less able children, write a group story using the Shared Writing scenario which you plan with them, i.e. plan and write chapters one by one.

The Ten-Question Guide

1. What type of story will it be?

2. Who is going to be in the story?

3. What is the setting? (Time and place)

4. Will it change?

5. Who is telling the story?

6. How does the story open?

7. What is the initiating event?

8. What happens as a result?

9. How is the situation resolved?

10. How will the story end?

Event		
Characters		
Theme		
Style		
Language		
Appeal		

Fantasy stories are about things that cannot really happen or about people or creatures who do not exist.

- They can be set in any time period

- Events can take place in:
  - the real world
  - an imaginary world modelled closely on the real world
  - a totally different imaginary world

- Characters can be:
  - ordinary humans
  - super-human (humans with special powers)
  - animals who talk and behave like humans
  - invented beings with human characteristics
  - invented creatures and monsters

- Fantasy stories are a mixture of the real and the unreal:
  - real people in the real world but with unreal events
  - real people getting into an unreal world
  - unreal characters (e.g. talking animals, ghosts) in the real world
  - real people in the real world but with time travel
  - unreal characters but speaking and acting as humans in an unreal world

- They can involve:
  - a journey or quest
  - good versus evil
  - magic
  - a fantasy solution to a real problem
  - scientifically advanced societies

Fantasy is anything that you can possibly imagine!

Chimney-sweep!

All the children started at Tom's dirty black figure – the girls began to cry, and the boys began to laugh, and all pointed at him rudely enough; but Tom was too tired to care for that.

"What art thou, and what dost want?" cried the old dame. "A chimney-sweep! Away with thee! I'll have no sweeps here."

Units of work 1–3 and 15

"Water," said poor Tom, quite faint.

"Water? There's plenty i' the beck," she said, quite sharply.

"But I can't get there; I'm most clemmed with hunger and drought." And Tom sank down upon the door-step, and laid his head against the post.

And the old dame looked at him through her spectacles one minute, and two, and three; and then she said, "He's sick and a bairn's a bairn, sweep or none."

"Water," said Tom.

Units of work 1–3 and 15

"God forgive me!" and she put by her spectacles, and rose, and came to Tom. "Water's bad for thee; I'll give thee milk." And she toddled off into the next room, and brought a cup of milk and a bit of bread.

Tom drank the milk off at one draught, and then looked up, revived.

"Where didst come from?" said the dame.

"Over Fell there," said Tom, and pointed up into the sky.

"Over Harthover? And down Lewthwaite Crag? Art sure thou art not lying?"

"Why should I?" said Tom, and leant his head against the post.

"And how got ye up there?"

Units of work 1–3 and 15

"I came over from the Place," and Tom was so tired and desperate he had no heart or time to think of a story, so he told all the truth in a few words.

"Bless thy little heart! And I'll warrant not. Why, God's guided the bairn, because he was innocent! Away from the Place, and over Harthover Fell, and down Lewthwaite Crag! Who ever heard the like, if God hadn't led him?"

Extract from *The Water Babies* by Charles Kingsley

Units of work 1–3 and 15

Planning a Story

Characters:
- A wizard
- His talking dog
- A girl

Setting:
- Time: the present
- Place: a street close to a school

Storyteller:
- The girl

Story Outline:
- Opening: girl is on her way to school and feeling very worried

- Initiating Event: she meets wizard and dog, explains she's not done her homework

- Action–Reaction: wizard suggests various rather silly solutions e.g. bus driver took it to wrap up his sandwiches; elephant took it to blow its nose

- Resolution: dog gets wizard to cast spell to make time go backwards 24 hours

- Ending: girl on way to school, thinking about that night's homework and decides: she'll do it before the TV film she wants to see? she'll watch TV instead and think of an excuse?

Units of work 4 and 5

Oberon's Magic

In another part of the forest, a workman called Bottom and his companions Snout and Quince are rehearsing for a play. Suddenly, Bottom becomes the victim of Oberon's magic. Oberon has changed Bottom's head into that of an ass (donkey). Bottom, however, does not realise what has happened.

SNOUT

O Bottom, thou art changed! What do I see on thee?

QUINCE

Bless thee, Bottom, bless thee! Thou art translated!

QUINCE and SNOUT run off.

translated changed

Unit of work 6

BOTTOM

I see their knavery: this is to make an ass of me, to fright me, if they could; but I will not stir from this place, do what they can. I will walk up and down here, and I will sing, that they shall hear I am not afraid.

BOTTOM sings.

TITANIA *(waking up)*

What angel wakes me from my
  flowery bed?
I pray thee, gentle mortal, sing again.
Mine ear is much enamoured of thy note;
So is mine eye enthrallèd to thy shape;

....

knavery trickery
enamoured enchanted
enthrallèd to thrilled by

Unit of work 6

And thy fair virtue's force perforce doth
  move me

On the first view, to say, to swear,
  I love thee.

> Titania tells Bottom that she loves
> him so much that he must stay with
> her in the wood. She calls four
> fairies – Peaseblossom, Cobweb,
> Moth and Mustardseed – to be
> Bottom's servants.

TITANIA *(turning to her fairies)*

Be kind and courteous to this gentleman;

Hop in his walks, and gambol in his eyes;

Feed him with apricots and dewberries,

With purple grapes, green figs and
  mulberries;

. . . .

hop in his walks, and gambol in his eyes
dance around him ready to serve him

Unit of work 6

The honeybags steal from the
humble-bees,
And for night tapers crop their
waxen thighs,
And light them at the fiery glow-worms'
eyes,
To have my love to bed, and to arise;
And pluck the wings from painted
butterflies
To fan the moonbeams from his
sleeping eyes;
Nod to him, elves, and do him courtesies.

Extract from *A Midsummer Night's Dream* by
William Shakespeare

. . . .

tapers candles
do him courtesies be very polite to him

Unit of work 6

Death of a Snowman

I was awake all night,

Big as a polar bear,

Strong and firm and white.

The tall black hat I wear

Was draped with ermine fur.

I felt so fit and well

Till the world began to stir

And the morning sun to swell.

I was tired, began to yawn;

At noon in the humming sun

I caught a severe warm;

My nose began to run.

My hat grew black and fell,

Was followed by my grey head.

There was no funeral bell,

But by tea-time I was dead.

Vernon Scannell

Unit of work 7

Bones!

"You've got bones on the brain. That's because you're a bonehead I suppose ..."

"But I tell you it's a real skellinton, Tyke. I tell you where I seen it. Down in the leat. I went there yesterday when you was out. Come on. Come and look. I bet it's somebody what's been murdered."

"I got into enough trouble over that marrow bone ..."

But Danny had set off along the road as if he was warming up for the fifteen hundred metres. He belted down the bank, where the old city walls stand, that drops down to the river and the

Unit of work 8

leats, the oldest part of the city, Sir says. I soon caught up with him, Crumble at my heels, her ears ruffling out in the wind.

"Which leat are the bones in?"

There are two, Cricklepit and Walter, that cut off from the river below the weir. The leats and the river make an island that's mostly a deserted place. Danny panted:

Unit of work 8

Pelican Shared Writing Fiction Teacher's Book Year 6 © Pearson Education Limited 2001

"By the bridge. Near the warehouses."

"They weren't there last week."

"The rain and high water brung
'em out."

We ran on, past the old, broken water-wheel, hidden in the trees and bushes, where the kingfisher flies sometimes. I've seen him quite a lot lately. I threw a broken brick into the water sluicing through an iron grid. The brown colour had gone but it was still high.

Pelican Shared Writing Fiction Teacher's Book Year 6 © Pearson Education Limited 2001

Everywhere was quiet. No one comes round here much. Everything's either being knocked down or rotting away; it's a place for secrets and adventures.

Perhaps this was an adventure. perhaps the bones were the skeleton of a murdered man, or valuable prehistoric remains.

Extract from *The Turbulent Term of Tyke Tyler* by Gene Kemp

Unit of work 8

A Flashback Story

Plot Outline

- A boy is thinking about something he has done wrong.
- He remembers how it all happened and how he has kept it to himself.
- Back in the present, he decides what he must do about it.

What the boy might have done:

Opening:

He watched the raindrops crawling their slow and miserable way down the window pane, echoing the way he was feeling. Like every other morning this week, in that quiet waking time before getting ready for school, he remembered.

Unit of work 9

Revising Your Writing

Story Structure:

- Have you made your settings clear?
- Do you have both main and secondary characters?
- Who is telling the story?
- Is your opening strong enough?
- What starts everything off? Is there a problem? Does something go wrong?
- What happens because of this?
- What is the high point of the action?
- How is the problem solved? What makes everything turn out right in the end?
- Is there a satisfying ending? Does the main character learn anything or change in any way?

Unit of work 10

Style:

Are there places where you could

- add words to make the meaning clearer or create detail?
- change words to be more exact or to have more effect?
- delete words to tighten things up?
- rearrange things to make better links, improve the flow or impact?
- alter sentence structures to improve and vary the writing?
- include similes and metaphors to improve descriptions?
- improve the punctuation to help the reader with the meaning?

Captain Hook's Plan

"I have often," said Smee, "noticed your strange dread of crocodiles."

"Not of crocodiles," Hook corrected him, "but of that one crocodile." He lowered his voice. "It liked my arm so much, Smee, that it has followed me ever since, from sea to sea and from land to land, licking its lips for the rest of me."

"In a way" said Smee, "it's a sort of compliment."

"I want no such compliments," Hook barked petulantly. "I want Peter Pan, who first gave the brute its taste for me."

He sat down on a large mushroom, and now there was a quiver in his voice.

Unit of work 11

"Smee," he said huskily, "that crocodile would have had me before this, but by a lucky chance it swallowed a clock which goes tick tick inside it, and so before it can reach me I hear the tick and bolt." He laughed but in a hollow way.

"Some day," said Smee, "the clock will run down, and then he'll get you."

Hook wetted his dry lips. "Aye," he said, "that's the fear that haunts me."

Since sitting down he had felt curiously warm. "Smee," he said, "this seat is hot." He jumped up. "Odds bobs, hammer and tongs, I'm burning."

They examined the mushroom, which was of a size and solidity unknown on the mainland; they tried to pull it up, and it came away at once in their hands, for it had no root. Stranger still, smoke began at once to ascend. The pirates looked at each other. "A chimney!" they both exclaimed.

Unit of work 11

They had indeed discovered the chimney of the home under the ground. It was the custom of the boys to stop it with a mushroom when enemies were in the neighbourhood.

Not only smoke came out of it. There came also children's voices, for so safe did the boys feel in their hiding-place that they were gaily chattering. The pirates listened grimly, and then replaced the mushroom. They looked around them and noted the holes in the seven trees.

"Did you hear them say Peter Pan's from home?" Smee whispered, fidgeting with Johnny Corkscrew.

Hook nodded. He stood for a long time lost in thought, and at last a curdling smile lit up his swarthy face. Smee had been waiting for it. "Unrip your plan, captain," he cried eagerly.

"To return to the ship," Hook replied slowly through his teeth, "and cook a large rich cake of a jolly thickness with green sugar on it. There can be but one room below, for there is but one chimney. The silly moles had not the sense to see that they did not need a door apiece. That shows they have no mother. We will leave the cake on the shore of the mermaids' lagoon. These boys are always swimming about there, playing with the mermaids.

Unit of work 11

They will find the cake and they will gobble it up, because, having no mother, they don't know how dangerous 'tis to eat rich damp cake." He burst into laughter, not hollow laughter now, but honest laughter. "Aha, they will die."

Smee had listened with growing admiration.

"It's the wickedest, prettiest policy ever I heard of," he cried.

Extract from *Peter Pan* by J. M. Barrie

Unit of work 11

Ute Prayer

Earth teach me stillness

as the grasses are stilled with light.

Earth teach me suffering

as old stones suffer with memory.

Earth teach me humility

as blossoms are humble with
beginning.

Earth teach me caring

as the mother who secures her young.

Earth teach me courage

as the tree which stands all alone.

Earth teach me limitation

as the ant which crawls on the ground.

Unit of work 12

Earth teach me freedom

as the eagle which soars in the sky.

Earth teach me resignation

as the leaves which die in the fall.

Earth teach me regeneration

as the seed which rises in the spring.

Earth teach me to forget my self

as melted snow forgets its life.

Earth teach me to remember kindness

as dry fields weep with rain.

Traditional Ute (North America)

Unit of work 12

Meeting

"Yes," said Tom bluntly, on opening the front door. "What d'you want?"

A harassed middle-aged woman in a green coat and felt hat stood on his step. He glanced at the armband on her sleeve. She gave him an awkward smile.

"I'm the Billeting Officer for this area," she began.

"Oh yes, and what's that got to do wi' me?"

She flushed slightly. "Well, Mr, Mr..."

"Oakley. Thomas Oakley."

"Ah, thank you, Mr Oakley." She paused and took a deep breath. "Mr Oakley, with the declaration of war imminent..."

Tom waved his hand. "I knows all that. Git to the point. What d'you want?" He noticed a small boy at her side.

"It's him I've come about," she said. "I'm on my way to your village hall with the others."

"What others?"

She stepped to one side. Behind the large iron gate which stood at the end of the graveyard were a small group of children. Many of them were filthy and very poorly clad. Only a handful had a blazer or coat. They all looked bewildered and exhausted. One tiny dark-haired girl in the front was hanging firmly on to a new teddy-bear.

The woman touched the boy at her side and pushed him forward.

"There's no need to tell me," said Tom. "It's obligatory and it's for the war effort."

"You are entitled to choose your child, I know," began the woman apologetically.

Tom gave a snort.

Units of work 13, 14 and 15

"But," she continued. "his mother wants him to be with someone who's religious or near a church. She was quite adamant. Said she would only let him be evacuated if he was."

"Was what?" asked Tom impatiently.

"Near a church."

Tom took a second look at the child. The boy was thin and sickly-looking, pale with limp sandy hair and dull grey eyes.

"His name's Willie," said the woman.

Willie, who had been staring at the ground, looked up. Round his neck, hanging from a piece of string, was a cardboard label. It read "William Beech".

Units of work 13, 14 and 15

Tom was well into his sixties, a healthy, robust, stockily-built man with a head of thick white hair. Although he was of average height, in Willie's eyes he was a towering giant with skin like coarse, wrinkled brown paper and a voice like thunder.

He glared at Willie. "You'd best come in," he said abruptly.

Extract from *Goodnight Mr Tom* by Michelle Magorian

Units of work 13, 14 and 15

Pelican Shared Writing Fiction Teacher's Book Year 6 © Pearson Education Limited 2001

The River Cinquains

Morning

Moorland:

Purple heather.

Early sun lights the stream:

Rushing, chattering, swift with fish,

Sparkling.

Afternoon

Townscape:

Water reflects

Grey brickwork, dull windows.

Fishermen stare. The river moves

Slowly.

Evening
Salt-marsh:
Under lead skies
The water slides away
From the damp banks of sand a few
Birds call.

Nigel Cox

Unit of work 16

Reunion

Lena's family were moved to many different camps during the war. Her father was separated from them and they have not seen him for several years. The war is now over...

Back at the camp our mother was hunting for us. "Where have you been?" she asked me. "And where is your sister?" And her voice was as shrill as the wind through the cracks in the walls of our hut.

The snow came down in the night and in the morning all the valley was white and hushed. Then over the mountainside we could see the first of the searching

Pelican Shared Writing Fiction Teacher's Book Year 6 © Pearson Education Limited 2001

people for the day arriving, coming down the slope like ants. And suddenly across the snow I could hear a mouth-organ.

"It's Father!" I called.

And I ran. And ran. Shouting. Falling in the snow drifts. Laughing. Crying. I was the first to reach him. And he hugged me. And hugged me. And hugged me.

Pelican Shared Writing Fiction Teacher's Book Year 6 © Pearson Education Limited 2001

Then my sister came. And he hugged her.

And my mother. And they hugged
each other.

And we all hugged each other.

Till Father said, "Careful. We don't want
to break the other wing".

And he pulled something out of his pocket. I thought it would be a bird – a blue tit or a goldfinch.

But it was a fragment of glass. And in the glass there was an angel. Blue as the sky and gold as the Sun.

My sister fingered the sharp edges. "Its wing is broken," she said sadly.

"But look!" I said. "It's playing a mouth-organ!"

"You could say so," Father laughed.

"Where did you find it?" Mother asked.

"In the ruins of a church," Father said. "And it's kept me company all the time I've been searching for you."

"And how did you find us?"

Father laughed again. "Whenever I went into a camp, I played my mouth-organ. And children used to come up to me and say, 'Those are the songs Lena and Anna used to sing. You must be their father. They said you had one arm and played the mouth-organ.' So I knew I'd find you somewhere, some day."

My sister said, "Can we go home now?" And our mother asked it with her eyes.

But our father shook his head. "There's no home to go to. And other people have taken our land."

Units of work 17, 18 and 19

My sister said, "It's not fair. After everything..."

But our father put his mouth-organ to her lips and her words turned into funny sounds. And we all laughed.

"We'll find another home," our father said. "You'll see."

And we did. Though it took a long while...

Extract from *The Angel With a Mouth Organ* by Christobel Mattingley

Units of work 17, 18 and 19

Strange Meeting

Story Genre: Fantasy

Chapter 1 Introduce setting and main character (who has a problem?)

Chapter 2 Meets someone by chance

Chapter 3 A journey – where? How?

Chapter 4

Unit of work 20